When I'm At Work

Firefighter

Written by Sue Barraclough
Photography by Chris Fairclough

W
FRANKLIN WATTS

First published in 2005 by Franklin Watts
338 Euston Road, London NW1 3BH

Franklin Watts Australia
Level 17/207 Kent Street
Sydney NSW 2000

© Franklin Watts 2005

Editors: Caryn Jenner, Sarah Ridley
Designer: Jemima Lumley
Art direction: Jonathan Hair
Photography: Chris Fairclough

With thanks to Racheal Sergeant, Michael Murphy and other
members of the Red Watch at Chiswick Fire Station for their
assistance with this book. Also thanks to Arun and Nathan
Holloway and Sonny Vincent for agreeing to appear in the book.

A CIP catalogue record for this book is available from the
British Library

ISBN 978 0 7496 6052 9

Dewey decimal classification number: 363.37'8

Printed in China

Franklin Watts is a division of Hachette Children's Books,
an Hachette Livre UK company.

Contents

I am a firefighter

My name is Racheal and I work at a fire station in London.

I am part of a team of firefighters
and my team is called Red Watch.
We start work with a parade when
we are given our duties for the day.

Checking the equipment

We check the equipment every
morning and after each call-out.
Everything must be working properly.

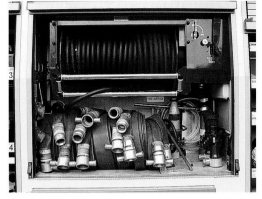

All the equipment is stored in the fire engine. Everything has to be put away in the right place so we can find it again easily.

In the office

CHISWICK

RED WATCH

ROLL CALL BOARD

DATE : 19 SEPT   1st DAY/NIGHT

WATCHROOM	Sub O	MURPHY		✓
FF WATKINS SARGEANT	LFF	MURRAY	MD (EL)	✓
PUMP LADDER				
Sub.O MURPHY	FF	HASTINGS	MD (EL) FRU-UR	AL
FF MURRAY				
LFF MURRAY	FF	KELLY	MD-(EL)	✓
FF SARGEANT	FF	GLANCY		✓
FF WATKINS				
FF GLANCY	FF	LANGFORD		✓
BA LORRY				
FF KELLY	FF	SANDERS		LSL
FF				
BATTERIES FF GLANCY	FF	SARGEANT		✓
ECO FF GLANCY				
AVAILABLE FF LANGFORD	FF	WATKINS		✓
FF				
MESS MANAGER FF LANGFORD	REQUIRED			
MESS ASSISTANT FF	REQUESTS			

We take it in turns to keep
careful records of who
is on duty.

10

In the office there is a teleprinter. This prints out details of each emergency. We choose the correct map from the drawer so we know where to go.

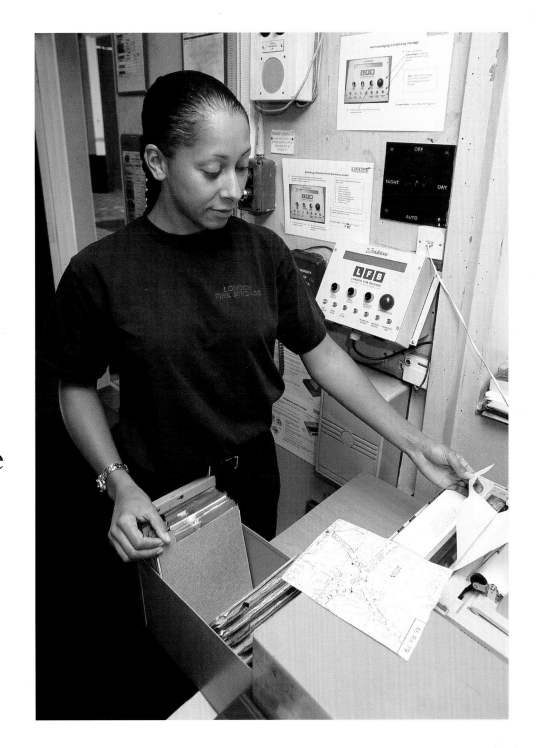

The alarm sounds!

When the alarm sounds we have to get to the fire engine as quickly as possible. If I am upstairs, I slide down a pole.

We put on our jackets, trousers and boots fast!

We climb into the fire engine
and put on our seat belts.
The lights flash and the siren
blares as we leave the fire station.

Working as a team

We have regular drills at the station.
We practise using all our equipment so that
we work together well in an emergency.

Practising skills

The fire station has a tall tower
so that we can practise climbing
into tall buildings.

We pull the hose up using ropes, then we tie it in place. The hose is heavy when it is full of water.

Breathing apparatus

If I go into a smoky building I wear breathing apparatus.
I carry a tank of air on my back.

A safety officer keeps a record
of who goes into the building.

Road accidents

Firefighting is not the only job we do. Sometimes we are called to road accidents to help people who are trapped in their cars.

We have special equipment that
cuts through metal and glass.
Then we can get people out safely.

Welcoming visitors

Sometimes groups of children come to the fire station.

Arun is sitting in our fire engine and Nathan is trying out the radio. Sonny is finding out how to use the hose.

Change of watch

When we have finished work, another team called White Watch arrives to take over. There is always someone on duty at the fire station, day and night.

After the handover parade,
I am off duty and I can go home.

Firefighting equipment

Firefighters keep their **uniforms** in one place. The boots and trousers are left together so that they are easy to pull on quickly.

A firefighter's **torch** is clipped to to the front of the jacket so it can be used hands-free.

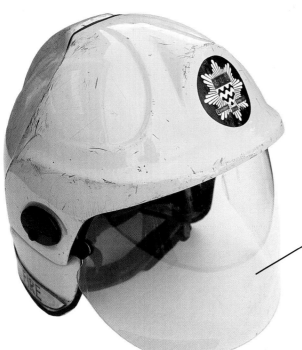

The **helmet** protects a firefighter's head. The visor can be pulled down to protect the face and eyes.

visor

lever

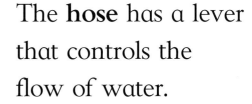

Firefighters' **gloves** are made from tough, heat-resistant material.

The **hose** has a lever that controls the flow of water.

Fire safety and prevention

It is important to talk with your family about what you would do if there was a fire in your home. Make an escape plan so you can get out as quickly as possible in an emergency.

- Don't leave toys or clothes near fires or heaters.
- Don't play near fires or heaters.
- Don't play with matches or lighters.

If there is a fire:

Get out

Stay out

and call 999

Ask your parents to fit a smoke alarm with the British Standard kitemark. The best place to install an alarm is on the ceiling in the centre of the room or hallway. If your home has more than one level, fit an alarm on each one. Test the alarm regularly and change the battery every year.

Smoke alarms save lives.

Glossary and index

breathing apparatus - a face mask joined to an oxygen tank. **Page 18**

call-out - a message calling for help. **Page 8**

drill - a training exercise. **Page 14**

duties - the things you need to do as part of your job. **Page 7**

on duty - working at your job. **Pages 10, 24**

parade - an inspection line. **Pages 7, 25**

records - information that is written down. **Pages 10, 19**

team - a group of people who work together. **Pages 7, 14, 24**

teleprinter - a machine that receives and sends typed messages. **Page 11**

watch - the group of firefighters on duty at a particular time. **Pages 7, 24**